Baba, the Farmer

Written and Illustrated by **Karen Johnson**

Proofreader **Barbara-Ann Jennings**

AuthorHouse™
1663 Liberty Drive
Bloomington, IN 47403
www.authorhouse.com
Phone: 1 (800) 839-8640

Published by AuthorHouse 09/12/2019

ISBN: 978-1-5049-3067-3 (sc)
ISBN: 978-1-7283-2741-9 (hc)
ISBN: 978-1-5049-3068-0 (e)

Library of Congress Control Number: 2015913323

Print information available on the last page.

authorHOUSE®

To TaMari D, Johnson (Granddaughter)

Real Stories from the Heart

I give thanks for the sun that rises, I give thanks for the rain that falls, I give thanks for the seeds I've sown that they grow, grow, and grow.

I give thanks for the sun that rises, I give thanks for the rain that falls, I give thanks for the seeds I've sown that they grow, grow, and grow

Baba is a farmer and a father of five sons who sang the song each morning before going into the field to work. Baba taught each of his sons that when you rise each morning give thanks and sing this song.

Baba would rise up early each morning and give thanks for the new day. He would meditate in the word and pray then; he would start to sing the song, while he washed up and dressed for the day.

His boys knew it was soon time for them to get up, because Baba was singing the song all through the house. Baba would go to the kitchen, start a pot of coffee and pour a glass of orange juice. Baba was a happy father and each note of the song echoed delightfully. Each of the boys would get up starting with the oldest, following Baba's song into the kitchen.

The boys would help prepare the breakfast. Baba's youngest son would come into the kitchen last, singing that song as he joined his father. They would all sit at the table together and have breakfast; Baba giving thanks for the food they ate.

At the breakfast table, Baba would go over the daily duties. When Baba finished giving out the chores, the rooster was crowing and Baba headed out the door singing his song.

I give thanks for the sun that rises, I give thanks for the rain that falls, I give thanks for the seeds I've sown that they grow, grow, and grow.
I give thanks for the sun that rises, I give thanks for the rain that falls, I give thanks for the seeds I've sown that they grow, grow, and grow.

Baba would work all morning long singing that song, going from one field to the next crop. Baba had a large variety of vegetables; Corn, String Beans, lentils, Sweet Potatoes, White Potatoes, Cabbages, Cauliflower, broccoli, Brussels sprouts, Onions and

Garlic, Spinach, Sweet Peas, Carrots; Squash, Beets, Bell Peppers red, green and yellow. Baba had Tomatoes, Eggplants, Cucumber and Lettuce. Baba also had a variety of fruits Strawberries, Berries, Peaches, Pears, Watermelon, Cantaloupe and Pumpkin. Baba was pleased with his crops, each year his crops thrived and flourished.

Every year the village and town would gather for the harvest festival, where contests were held for the best crops. Baba sowed fields that yielded a fruitful harvest. Each year he won the harvest festival challenge with the first place rewards. Many felt Baba was humble and considered him a wise upright and blessed man. While working he continued singing his song.

Yes, we give thanks for the sun that rises, we give thanks for the rain that falls, and we give thanks for the seeds we've sown that they grow, grow and grow.

Yes, we give thanks for the sun that rises, we give thanks for the rain that falls, and we give thanks for the seeds we've sown that they grow, grow and grow.

Baba had worked long and hard that day, and at the end of the day, grew very tired. He headed home and cleaned up for the evening meal. After dinner, Baba meditated and gave thanks; then retired early to bed. The following morning Baba got up, meditated, gave thanks and began to sing his song.

Baba stopped singing his song and went back into his room and got into bed. He wasn't feeling well. His oldest son noticed the song wasn't echoing throughout the house. He got up and went to check on Baba and asked him if he was feeling alright. Baba said, "Not today son, not at all." "You'll have to take charge and over see the chores." Each of the other four sons was awakened by still quiet house, and arose to also check on Baba. The oldest son explained that Baba didn't feel well this morning and that they would have to work all the chores together.

The boys prepared for the day with breakfast, and then went over the chores. The oldest said, "I will go into town and seek the Doctor for a remedy."The second and third oldest boys will go to the market place to sell are vegetables. The fourth oldest son will stay here and look after Baba and prepare the meals. The youngest son will work the farm chores. The youngest son said, "How will I work the farm by myself?" and all four brothers cried out the way Baba taught you!!

Each of the brothers headed off on their way, the youngest brother went to his room for a moment, when he came out he began to sing the song.

Yes, we give thanks for the sun that rises, we give thanks for the rain that falls, and we give thanks for the seeds we've sown that they grow, grow and grow. Yes, we give thanks for the sun that rises, we give thanks for the rain that falls, and we give thanks for the seeds we've sown that they grow, grow and grow.

He went out into the fields and checked on each crops, plucking weeds, turning vegetables over; inspecting the growth; he went over each of the vegetables; then he went and checked on the fruits, all the while singing that song.

He sang that song every way he could, and with Baba on his mind, he was reminded of every step that Baba did when he was in the field working. The young brother worked hard and before he realized it the farm chores were done. While walking to the house, he sang the song.

At the end of the day, Baba's other sons reached the grounds. As they were walking up the road, they took notice of the fields and crops. They said their youngest brother did a good job. When the boys reached the house, all five were standing on the porch.

The oldest brother told the youngest brother he did a good job in the field; and, asked how he did it. The youngest son said, "The way Baba taught me, and began to sing Baba's song. All of the brothers joined in singing.

Yes, we give thanks for the sun that rises, we give thanks for the rain that falls, and we give thanks for the seeds we've sown that they grow, grow and grow. Yes, we give thanks for the sun that rises, we give thanks for the rain that falls, and we give thanks for the seeds we've sown that they grow, grow and grow

Then they laughed and smiled at each other. Suddenly, they heard a single voice echoing throughout the house growing louder as it reached the door

Yes, we give thanks for the sun that rises, we give thanks for the rain that falls, and we give thanks for the seeds we've sown that they grow, grow and grow

The boys cried out, "Baba!! You're feeling better". And Baba said, "Yes, I do and I see that you boys have all grow", grow" and grow".

Yes, we give thanks for the sun that rises, we give thanks for the rain that falls, and we give thanks for the seeds we've sown that they grow, grow and grow.

Yes, we give thanks for the sun that rises, we give thanks for the rain that falls, and we give thanks for the seeds we've sown that they grow, grow and grow.
Yes, we give thanks for the sun that rises, we give thanks for the rain that falls, and we give thanks for the seeds we've sown that they grow, grow and grow.

Yes, we give thanks for the sun that rises, we give thanks for the rain that falls, and we give thanks for the seeds we sown that they grow, grow and grow.

Baba The Farmer

NOTE: on farming Volume of water irrigation Agriculture the volume of water needed to irrigate an area of land in order to cultivate a crop for planting to harvest
Allocated task; a task or service allocated to somebody especially in the course of work. Baba produces leadership at each harvest
Nutrition with variety of vegetables

Written by Karen M. Johnson
Children Story
Part of the Creative Storytelling